Porch Light

By the same author

Incidental Complications

Porch Light

Ivy Ireland

PUNCHER & WATTMANN

First published in 2015

Published by Puncher and Wattmann
PO Box 441
Glebe NSW 2037

http://www.puncherandwattmann.com
puncherandwattmann@bigpond.com

National Library of Australia
Cataloguing-in-Publication entry:

Ireland, Ivy

Porch Light

ISBN   9781922186713

I. Title.

A821.3

Cover design by Matthew Holt
Printed by McPherson's Printing Group

This project has been assisted by the
Australian Government through the
Australia Council, its arts funding and
advisory body.

Australian Government

Australia Council
for the Arts

Contents

Space Opera

Follies

for Murrie

Space Opera

Porch Light

'How do the angels get to sleep when the Devil leaves the porch light on?'
— Tom Waits

1.

If you consulted your own cipher-mind (if what presents as yours could be
compressed in such a lazy line), would it encircle this whole ball of string
    theory
or only what lies beneath? Every oceanic floor peak, all those pre-lung
beasts that beckon us back, ever back, while we struggle up here in the
arc of your earth-wing? It is suffocating under your airs, Old Birdman,
we don't know enough about our own night terrors to ever consider yours.
To claim you frighten the children with your silent staring is like
naming the midnight ocean mysterious, to sing out your secret symbol
through all this typical cataclysm might boil our blood.
Still, see you slip and slide out of heaven into the foam pits of human love:
more, elevated, other. Exotic, no matter how well disguised, for we
blinks of one of your manifold eyes don't claim to tune into our own
    timings.
There is a connection octave-plinking through this mystical equation,
yet this is not another symposium examining the intricacies of angels.

2.

Perhaps some planet put you up to it. You didn't want so many eyes on your
    wings:
it's embarrassing, it's a job. Hard to refigure you without, yet once in the
annals of this endless processing, perhaps you were writ down as feather-
    skin, transitional form.
If only we had come down from the birds, we too could be haunted by
    memory of flight.

We did not fling down from the firmament; we squelched up from watery
depths, aquatic apes. You are a terraform failure. Fire-sword bearing man-
birds could have ruled, yet water monkeys made it through. Your trajectory,
defeated, exited earth for heaven. The fall went up. You did not
win. We did not rejoice in the progression.
This murky wet won't leave us – even now we are swamp and slime. You:
air or light or both, descend on passage-ladders right before our very minds.
We grasp hold of the base, steady it with a sick grin. You can at
least go back up the way you came down.
We can never return; we left our gills on the shore and the tide snatched
    them back.
If we, green with envy or slime, are seeking Return, it is to pond and
    puddle;
yours is to some flaming red aerial heart of everything.

3.

You cut the fancy-free heart right out of us. In the witching hours, when
night dervish morphs into night mare, you are stilled, silenced, scribbling
    and scribing, saving it all
up to sing it out later. Some Lizard-God wants to know the electro-
magnetic reading of an attempt at meeting. Circling the throne, later and
always reporting, you proclaim the heart to be still beating – that pink-to-
    blue mass, alone in the shadow of all horrors,
what can go on between lovers: smashed telephones, shared appliances,
night. Watcher, you are never still, you whisper continuum to these
moments even as you raise the knife. Left to our own devices, we could be
the scribes of our own autopsy, the records of entanglement's dissection.
We could carve up the shared ventricles, the cleft aorta,
discover what was never beating to begin with. We could bathe our empty
    cavity in a
plenty-more-fish sea, decide what cut out means, what we will do with the
etch-mark-once-heart, what new world our new work will break forth into.

But with you here, light bleeds along the wall, the shuddering is of
presence and we know − clinging and ejecting aside no matter on whose
    behalf − we are poppets.

4.

You burst forth as a woman. We thought this soft body too moist to house
an angel. Murky spirits aplenty, but pure swords of light? When the
    Heavenly Grace stabs in,
it will leak out through all those holes. To where will it escape? How will
we find it all to shove it back in again? We saw those frescos, believed
    them, for they were birthed out of
Holy Father. The Devil with breasts, leaking out everywhere to all sorts:
constantly shadow, probably dark matter and other arcane fears of science.
We suppose you could be our Mother, angel, you are cold and removed, set
in marble. Yet we overlooked you for centuries, you were so far away, and
    we certainly forgot
you could possibly be true, what with all that loft and strength and absence.
Isn't absence of the father? If you were allowed to choose,
you might seek woman out because here we seek out our names through
    pain.
You want your own gender angst, a category other to Holy. We won't tell,
we will watch you watching us as you reflect sheen on this Leviathan's
    back,
drag the frescos towards your breast for spring clearing, a bath in new
    light.

5.

Blood. You are out for it, we try to keep it in, at all costs. Blood:
The way to tell if we are here or not is whether we can hear it circling. Or
    not.
It's unlovable, really. It is smelly and of metal and is awfully difficult to

remove from cashmere once it all floods out. We are constantly managing it,
feeding it, giving it away, taking it all back. It's essentially a connector, even
    magnetic.
We wonder why you want to exchange pulsating white for toffee apple
    sticky.
We don't think you would if you really knew what it meant. Blood, Blut or
    Bloed,
might be our earliest word. It has always been there, unforeseeable just like
    you.
Blood is the very opposite of you: intermediary, link, vapid passageway.
Blood raises spirits and runs to the sacred places. Blood is in the family.
Anything but pallid, blood of an other contains your revenge. You can never
    have revenge, Watcher.
Say we don't know how lucky we are to own it, say what you will. We are
bloody-minded, moving onwards over bones that birthed the whole bloody
    mess is all we know.
Our red warmth runs cold against all your white. We have always been
    afraid of this.

6.

As the glory pours in and through, even the Throne of the Most High
is merely a tube. There are innumerable zillions even in our own brains
without considering the external piping we construct to extend the nexus
    out. To echo the universe, which is one
Giant Conduit sucking us all in, out, round and round, we recreate the
cylindrical vessel. Inside the spaces of subatomic nothings, how many
cylinders? We etch on the lining of a brain-tube while cannulas poison to
near-death, while lines to arms and throat and heart ensure life persists with
a tube no longer viable inside where evolution always requires it.
Inserted tubes suck out the pooled blood like pulped prayers. TV is The tube,
we yearn to recall when thrown out of your tunnel of Graceful Light, yet by
that time pain, and not-remembering, are the new profound. The nostril

tube floods oxygen,

floats brains so far away that blood-prayers creep in and add up

somewhere outside all tubing: the dark energy inside. Isn't it enough that
    you ensure our continuing?

That exploding would have burst all persistence even as we received The

Annunciation, sipping from a chipped teacup while scrawling the word
    'Grigori' at the top of the page.

7.

So hard to tell if the birds are mating or fighting. The koalas are
    attempting both,

here in last the pocket protected enough for them to keep at it. We too
    keep at it:

against, always against. It's not your fault, messenger, yours is to intone
    the Great Law.

The Great Law is Always. We are to blame – bifurcate is all we do down

here. Small wonder the axis teeters, unsure of whether to shift or remain

safe in stasis. It will break, this is Occam's Razor. Now, while our hair falls

out (it's the anaesthetic, it's the morphine), you gibber endlessly,
    something about the Great Glory, what was

before until then. As our wounds pus and blister, we grow tired of this

obfuscated babble. You are doing it deliberately, jiggling these
    abstractions, these meaning-carrots,

before our puny brains. Say what you mean to say, Watcher, is this

all? Here? This everymorning dying? Last koalas grunting in blind

continuing, whip birds and koels bouncing beckon or warning against the

everywhere-everything hills. Clouds so sneaky, when we turn our backs

the sky is something else entirely. Light on new leaf, trembling. You

gibbering on, some non-direction-everywhere, while our best awe is
    silence.

Waxing Moon in Virgo

Lone magpie cry against morning.
Sometimes you implode inside to experience it:
galaxy upon galaxy of no new Earth,
all alone against the colossal empty.

You think colossal empty and are proud of it,
as though the real fears could be quantified,
and, once named, obliterated by word-magic —
as though dying to it all was ever enough.

Dying is enough, yet you refute the finer points,
so this forfeiture continues.

This one is dying, this old Earth you loved,
part of you dares it to go.
Part of you must have sent it packing:
the mind is the Earth is the mind.

Grinning, because even in the leather of all this ending,
the animal continues, the colossal empty still grants boons;
magpie song still drowns out the tick of continuing,
sunrise still enters with black tea. Perhaps ginger.

High Tea with the Muse

If you do not arrive
I will leave this birdless space,
eject all useless speech,
turns of phrase, say:

'Silence. Increased silence.
Stilled sea. Not a pin drop.
Not one.'

Then laughter
– your laughter –
will begin.

I remain here at the
base of things, waiting.
I am left here at the primal seed,
needing to thread

one white teapot,
two silver spoons,
two patterned teacups

through the blanket of where things are,
where things should be,
where you might pop up:

no blame.
This vase in the kitchen holds
six blue flowers,
fresh oranges are cut into quarters,

there could be endless top-ups of tea.

If you were here with me,
I could slip, slow, inside,
Beg the birds' return, write:

dancing in the circus of circumstance,
married to movement's minutiae:
mindlessness of mind.

Equilibrium

'The work of God is done in an instant'
— Antoine-Joseph Pernety

The winged tiny thing nibbling
skin, no,
salt from this skin,
can have its fill,
while a lion doing similar
will necessarily be denied.

You, situated somewhere
in the food chain
— midpoint —
between beetles and sharks,
may take only what is yours
from what is mine,
and I'll have what's mine from you.
This exchange is still sanctified (even now);
All will no doubt follow suit.

In our process of equilibrium,
we extract art from primal matter,
ferment these mercurial waters
with the sulphur of self-sacrifice.
Love, the endpoint, is the only elixir:

as precious as the pause
between wing beats,
as seamless as the glint
that marries sky to sea.

Uncreation

I swear to you it was because she wanted release.
There was this hold on things; a gravity; a grandeur.
There was this cosmological constant
inconsistent with all we know about Law.

There was nothing else for it, I swear. She bit her lip,
fired.

And then this blaze on things.
And then the surprised squeal from things being illuminated,
displayed without their
bits on.

There was pause,
a hideous silence.

I promise you it was because she wanted to exhale,
give back the primal matter,
witness process: everything nullifying
everything else out, all becoming ether;
nobody getting what they want,
all appeased with fog-phantoms of near-enough,
homogeneous sublimation.

She told herself it wasn't happening,
that she didn't start the whole thing,
that the arrow of time was something she made up
to get the kids to bed.

I swear to you it wasn't her fault – she was the point at which
infinity found its rest,
the center of a black hole
in which relativity and probability combined peacefully.

I swear to you it was because there was a mistake in this method –
it had to be released. She lit the kiln,
temperature off the scale,
watched eternity cease,
the vessel implode.

Apocalypse in the Garden

A day. A forgotten myth day and all this
light: new glow on old leaf. The blip of
spring, inserting fierce will into every sad gap.

Old Father is anxious, and the Maiden:
golden horror. All this anticipation,
dangling comfort over the edges, accepting

half-breath in the place of utterance.
If there is a season in this almostness,
name it: pause, fissure. Say, "quashed frost."

Say what you will, these new bush vines reach
towards, only towards — they know what death
moves backwards from before to join them here.

This fresh strength of sun, more brawny every year,
is fuelled by blank stare, forced eye-meets, the last thing
you ever want to take in, here at the natural end.

What we do for Survival

For Jon Catapan's Body Chart, Newcastle Region Art Gallery

Green was first when the extant set out to condense itself down.
Then cinnabar: capillaries of fire and endlessness,
a nest of triangles, symbols of the Three Principles —
the Great Heart of some elapsed thing.

The only world we can cope with
is this shopping list of perceptions:
round bottomed flask, orphic egg,
Aurora Australis, lung sack,
runes in cubes seeming to square the circle,
Tetragrammaton in a cyclic continuum
trailing off the canvas, off this Perspex page.

Consciousness is not the only node
responding to this inoculation of meaning —
the body catches the flame, also.
Electrical signals smelt biology and chemistry
from shamanism and alchemy,
distil human genome research from arcane pixels,
coagulate white noise with all this green-black rapid change.

What lies beneath this ladder of coercion
is still beneath;
scumble-over it as we will,
set it free though we may.

Fly Away After Kandinsky

it was not painted for you
so don't explain this
inherent linking
ask it to please leave
yet still some shade remains
when you close your lids
you couldn't be crazed
enough to take a photo
still these dots keep forming
everything into nothing
congratulating their own
potential for raw image
revisiting a new light
it is not even Kandinsky's
ink anymore it is your own
lens and this new mistake
staring out over and against
fierce internal layering

Push: Sylvie Guillem & Russell Maliphant

don't dim the lights
for the stroking dark
will smother me also

light derails
silhouettes remain to
recreate fission

liquid she
while he is
pure chord

so much dissipation in together
as though one more leaning inwards
would shatter the whole thing

explode those jiggling bones
enforce gender collapse
make something somewhere please

the analogy is to raw element but also to
meeting complex self again and again
in and through these outward signs

some grasping after capture
wanting to write out the body
while knowing letters

will not even brush up against
the way dance leans towards
eternity every single time

what can you possibly say
sinew in calico
shadow on screen

constantly switched on to reveal
meat, guts and skin twisting
another idea back on itself

The Tunguska Event

All is observation and experiment.
God is blue and smells of bones
claims one who met with it,
others blame green aliens.

The law of inertia: a moving object
will preserve its velocity and direction
until something influences it
out of its path.

A fireball hitting Siberia, June 30th 1908,
instead moves forests from its path,
produces an atmospheric shockwave
that circles the earth, twice.

In London, ten thousand kilometres away,
for two whole days and nights,
a newspaper can be read at any hour
down any un-lamped lane.

Through the light-adhering qualities of
atmospheric dust, there is no night.
What sets us neatly off course then-there,
provides a good mystery to rehash here.

We know well this magic:
mini shockwaves resonate still
in our own air, lungs, heart –
we are now made of this same dust.

We sense conspiracy: something ten
thousand times worse than the A-bomb,
perhaps anti-matter anti-exploding,
or Nikola Tesla shooting some

white flame stolen from a black hole
through earth, leaving only entry wounds.
No evidence was gathered, they were too
busy backing war to bother filing phenomena.

Tunguska, 1908. The Tsar leaves peasants,
town, eighty million trees to be obliterated,
blame their own blue gods, lie as powdered
bones while the future dreams up green aliens.

Venus Transits

We all know that your emergent seduction is
wind that whips and whirls through
airs bitter and fast enough to tear
heads off, not that your acid clouds wouldn't
melt off our best lead helmets before that
zephyr-guillotining had a chance to occur.
Let's not forget the constant impossible lightening.

Yet for eons, we peered out at you and saw
love, fertility, transcendent sex –
hopefully with your Botticelli –
all the endless wars necessary to achieve that end.
If only we could have grasped the semiotics when we
named you Beauty (it might mean the holy terror
inherent in the curious choices of combining elements).

Venus, your ins and outs fill our britches with scorpions.
For my part, I can only petition that your
sweet-and-sour stench will one day wash off;
this symbolism is far too sinister
to ever be fully grasped and defined
while we live altogether alone out here
against the secrets of our bodies.

This or that love you make generally causes death,
specifically causes death on the odd occasion,
inevitably causes death in French.
Upon reflection, and though it is utterly useless to do so,
I might well hate you, Venus,
as I spend this rough moment pondering
the dark sincerity of that hook in your belly.

I'm told that if I pray to you, sincerely,
you might remove the veils, one by one.
The veils are what we cannot see,
but which own our longings, regardless.
Gossamer gloaming films, made of ancient memory:
in our best moments we sense their presence in
that niggling cause for continuing psychotherapy.

What lies beyond your voluminous skirts
includes ten thousand more growing galaxies,
more revisions of deep time and Big History:
the past before any thinking on past,
the chronicle of silence and blackness;
that first tiny zero
endlessly liquid-papering itself out.

When you move across my surface, Venus,
I know to stay inside, draw the drapes tight,
chant Our Fathers, hide the mascara,
ask the neighbours, politely,
to bolt the door from the outside.
At least I should know to perform that ritual
by now. Thrice by thrice.

Still we all poke at you, through your cloud coverings,
revealing desertscape littered with calderas, yet no magma.
At the heart of all this faith and belief, love is volcanic winter.
We should learn to recall your deadlands, Venus,
those high-speed lead-melting acid-winds,
while engaging in soul-marriage or even
dud-night fornication with erstwhile rivals.

You force out exploration with your jaunts across our sun.
Lieutenant James Cook set out towards his own terrors,
determined to chart your black blimp against the
burning mass, take your true measure, thus ours,
even if it cost him his corneas,
even as it led to continuing genocide,
even though he never learned to swim.

Even today we are budding Cooks,
desiring to chart your extinct oceans, place floating pods
inside your sulphur droplets, that this thick fog might
hide from us your recently revealed fearful facade.
No landing explorer we have sponsored with our life-blood
has lasted more than an hour on your surface.
We would build air-cities, though we never learnt to fly.

When I watch you perform your transit trick now,
you appear practised and exact,
yet I know your clever movements cloak madness.
The way you capsize in our skies from dawn to dusk!
As though all that polarity we hold dear is nothing.
As though we, too, could quietly
flit out of our assigned archetypes, puddle into pure shadow.

Your flip-side guise is Mary, Mother of God:
high art aesthetics and high tea cakes:
decorous fruitfulness. We must make our offerings
to the dignified inside, yet I can't truly credit the
purity of your pastoral persona, Venus –
spring is much too terrifying
and motherhood, precarious.

Venus, you favour the time-between-times.
Teach us to be one thing and yet another mystery entirely.
Let us learn to navigate by your quixotic cycles,
that we might know what it means to campaign through
fire and that time before fire, and emerge,
ultimately understood in the afterglow:
a synthesis of self and shadow.

The Clearing

Today concerns the clearing of indifference:
flight on the horizon, the reaching after it involved,
that one sure math required to get us anywhere.

Then the great pause of intake:
the sugar of this golden finch,
these grasses slithering with spiders.

And those mountains, beloved, mountains!
Undersea, lurking where we will not
uncover their mysteries without the necessary history.

Or more special simplicities: things doing and undoing,
disguised as raw meat or not, enamoured or disgusted –
as I with you, as salt with heat.

To think we used to fear those pavement cracks.
Now we prod at them, romantic in volatility,
mythic in belligerence.

To think we used to sit with backs to the incoming comet,
eyes squished shut to the flashes in the corners,
the next ice age and the end of our form.

Now we allow a few clarifying blinks before
facing Armageddon. Now we reach through the clear
cold circumflex surrounding true sentience,

towards the veil that would cut us off, the great
gaping hole in that veil the last comet creates.
Now we gather lost fists together that used to shake at gods.

Gathering (it) Together

A dirt path through ghost gums; shadow-specked.
What is this loop extending out from your neck, pulling
forward, along, only to fold you back into your body again?

Whoosh of tiny wings,
brush of heavy skirts,
crunch of sun-baked clay.

Extending through all things, this endless loop:
entirety of infinite string theories
bifurcating off, gleaning further figure-eights,

returning you to source. You walk. A loop, only
visible through this dirt dervish with ghost gums,
reaches out, along, only to fold you back in again.

Strangler Fig

Seed dropped from some tarsus: careless.
It is a necessary thing, this taking-over —
sliding into the fork of some poor fortune's fool.

Elucidate for me this grasping, this clawing towards being,
this reach towards progeny at the cost of the host:
at the cost of any cost. Call it what you will.

Meanwhile, the seed thrives, cradled in the limbs of
the quarry. Gathered tulle roots slither out some
snake metamorphosis, as other mythical analogies

extend its magnificence so far up skyward.
Nothing if not breathtaking. In our glancing and gazing,
we forget it receives grandeur through murder.

Something in this smacks of ancient daemons we
called down to own us when our brain halves were still joined.
A necessary thing, this being taken-over: we now have iPhones.

First symbiosis, then slavery, then the necessary
cyclical sacrifice. Oh to become vessels again,
annihilate atomic structures, empty out. Can we, please?

Imagine digging into my veins, strangler fig,
finding a port for your primitive circulatory system,
adjusting your god-veins to the munificence of my viscera.

Imagine squeezing until I ceased true being,
became a rotted spine inside you: still mostly alive,
if life is the scientific definition we grant it.

Strangler fig, you are raw making and unmaking, right before our
eyes in this speck of rainforest the farms didn't inhale.
It is as inevitable as the giving out of ribs, this being taken-over.

Mangrove Sutra

Scrubby nothing, but for your aerial roots.
You know what it is to adapt against erosion,
guide the lone cell home. Through all tides, eons of celebrity,
calamity, love. If some holy soul granted me a catamaran or wings,
I, too, could further examine this line up of grubby snorkels,
the dark squelch of your stench. I, too, could hope for the
sudden growth of an external lung in all this tsunami sludge.

Pneumatophores (the God-adaption you grew when you could
no longer breathe through your green skin),
contain a moving-towards all things might undertake
against backwards, against re-visioning, against degeneration.
Yet here as humans, amidst all cyclical progression,
we still seek out some help outside ourselves to
block into this choreography; salvage the glory of our last pavane
before the entrance of whatever super-species comes next.

Your job is to hold back that tide that could kill us right now
as we sit here by the spa pool with our pina coladas.
Call you angel of the mud-squelch, the devil-dust of industry
clings to every puny chloroplast. It's like you simply remain
through epochs: slime to dinosaurs, ferns to figs –
and not much self-reflexive consciousness to be had in between.
There is something terrifying about your continuous primal narrative,
singing out against the technophiles and that toxic industry sludge
we are all so thick with down here by the docks.

Perhaps we all need aerial roots to suck in the god-mind far above,
rise up out of the murky gloom of inevitable progressions.
We would kill you off too, mangrove, yet I don't think we can:

you are more than us. We might be belligerent in our ignorance,
but you have practiced poise; demurring here with dignity
amongst these brash Styrofoam cups and piquant chip packets.
They will lie beside you – scrubby and awkward like you –
until the fat cherub blows that final feral note.

There's a clinging-to you hold dearly that we have no use for entirely.
Sentimental as we are, this endless leaving-off, moving on, letting
go is both our one true wish and only possible practice.
You, Methusela of the fringes, know what it is to live
beyond the bounds of the lease we forget we took out in the first place.
You challenge the demi-gods of robotics with your continuance.
A grove of you is a mangal: Indian for Lord, Sanskrit for Mars.
Perhaps we'll take you to zap the red planet with green, on our space ark,
when this whole vile earth affair is done with and forgotten about.

When we discovered your relics under the floor of the Great Barrier Reef,
in hiding from the last disaster, deep undersea branch systems
still intact from before a before we were around for,
we understood something casually, momentarily:
we just arrived here and still we will quit the sphere, perhaps prematurely,
perhaps deservedly. You, mangrove, will still be clawing your way through silt
when the next super-species finds our tomb, petrified, in the pith of the sea.

A Point in Space

things rising up and falling
over the end like a lone
white crane flying the last
brown stick into the final
sky so grey-blue-green
all would swear it was black
in the retellings of afterwards
supposing there was an afterwards

somehow I trip over
thus uncover
the end of the world rope
and it's not frayed like
previously considered
iniquitous hells or warrior heavens
it is diamond-cut severance
clean and faultless
even when observed under
an electron microscope
not one quark remains

and everything falls
out of the end
choice and chance
the mind
even paradox falls
off the end

it is not blackout or red-flash or
blanched silence
it is end
nothing to colour or be coloured
nothing to give colour a name
it is not even final

I see you there
constantly approaching
contemplating the structures we had
built-up to keep it all
downwind from where it ends
I say the way we thought backwards
keeping ideas of what went on here
safely in the dark of not enough sleep
you say futile
I say speaking of futile

I had been building for myself
for what would have felt like
forever had I not known end
a one out of the two of us
disregarding all others
it was as futile as
waiting for explanation

at the end
no triangles
no two of us
plus one ghost
not even one

I hope you saw then
why I could not comfort you
as you approached the end
as everything fell off of it
as you joined in the falling
as I could not yet

if there was to be a
recount of these events
if you had come
back from the end
you might have stated
something to soothe
you might have finally
turned to me then
you might have said —

Each Line

compare and contrast
reach of a pelican's neck against
constant comforting green

the stillness inside this road-kill crow
decomposing faster than you are — for now
from birth falling, dropping out of sky

each last line furthering the former
disregarding ending
racing endlessly towards, towards

grab a stick and say, forest, eden
use it as a warding rod
against the lines you are writing out

suggesting they were in, initially
a dog, perhaps three-headed and
certainly alarmingly large

grows tired of chasing sticks or lines
resumes guarding the door you can't see
though you sense it, entirely and always

a slavering three-headed dog not allowing
never allowing passage
until passage is all that is allowed

this is merely afternoon
the blurt of blowfly against gauze
those intersecting lines

crossing in, falling over fragments
for the bare brain to bear witness to
begin to seek to name

crow against dog
green against pelican
the drive on things to drop out of sky

in neat or messy lines,
sigh, name themselves
stick or Eden

Cancer

the exact date is
oak leaves in ice
explaining always
disregarding why
it can't possibly be
so still in here

when you want it
grace is oolong tea
bitter, warm – you
recall news backwards
even when wrangled with
a lingering word remains

and these ferns have
died for winter
you'd even prefer
your own miniature dog
over all these
emotional events

returning to slants
this possible c-word
now honest to god
stitching itself in as though
crumpling into the inevitable
would sort it all out

oak leaves in
cracked ice on
pond surface
or is it merely
another frozen puddle
this perfect fact
inside all rogue cells

Fission and Fusion

counting backwards from forever
a clock beneath all magma
cleaves to no metropolitan time zone
considers no adjustment for the glitch of axis

this symbolic regulator considers solely
the countless returns of hope
feeds eternity's frenzy with
the next bifurcation of chaos

nuclear physicists click over
our everyman clock
this doomsday clock to
nanoseconds off midnight

through the halls of the Orphic sanctuary
this molten core counter continues to fold
the knowledge of what follows over
the rune of when it all arrived

Wet Stockings

'Where does the other come from? Who is the other? I wear myself out, I shall
never know.' – Roland Barthes

Wet stocking clinging to my legs. Could remind me of the
big black vortex wrapped around this one small globe of light,
could even refer to my opaque analysis splayed carelessly
across your tepid sleep-form in the monsoon morning.

They almost hurt, the cling is so fierce.

Train-air adds a layer of ice to wet. Should've planned for this,
packed spare tights, an umbrella of arteries for when
the wet heart clogs itself with conclusions.
Mars could've given us neighbours, we wouldn't feel so drowned,

shivering out here in the great Earth-machine.

Out the window, the other is as impenetrable as the
cause that got me here: train air, wet legs, drawn conclusions –
the cogs of it all, endlessly colliding. Snack food
apocalypse: abandoned paper says there's an asteroid, waiting at 2012.

Travelling back in time, the other is nonplussed if my stockings are wet.

James Merrill House

Walking in (what is it our
antennae pick up really
do we even have antennae)
your legs give you heaps
yet you aren't nervous
what with the New England
pulpit preaching and the
shoreline public access path
closed due to ice. You are kept
safe, yet you could never be safe
with all these oak china cabinets.
But what would you know with
legs going loco, as though some
soul tugged at them, perhaps a
child expecting treats. What you
sought to discover was larger but
they took the art away because
it was all worth too much.
Here you forget he ever died as the
giant gold-framed photo in the
bat-infested lòunge room
(they didn't remove the wallpaper)
comes to life and dusts the willowware.
Perturbed, you sit down where you
should not and are promptly
scolded by your watchful guide
who is lovely but of course
yet tells you that gay men like
parlour games as though
this could dismiss any otherworlds

you might care to conjure up.
No, you are imagining things,
you can't be frowned upon, there is
now too much Botox in this glorious
fishing village, it's all a picture here
and besides, in summer shining
well-mannered children who aren't
ghosts eat ice-cream with
Truman Capote while their
genes dream of the glory days
they no doubt never had
back in ye Olde Englund.

Nuclear

In the dead centre of every last atom fragment is this O-gape hole,
void, empty. It's what the final A-bomb took when it ceased all future. No
going back now. All this sheer moving through time has to stop somewhere.
Can you tell me, light through variegated leaf, X-rayed by star radiation, to
    what
new portal the old light might move? As there is no possible response, let's
    limit
remarks to the weather: a perfect winter day, here in the land with no real
    cold left.
Out here in this garden, air so still one might almost hear the gas exchange:
carbon dioxide to oxygen and back again. There are always other elements,
some more sinister. Still, so much light and space, puny solar panels give
    out
more oomph than one small abode can handle. It's not so elsewhere, in the
dark, cold and ever-clouded winters, we unearth what probably should
    remain
earthed to make the heat-machines motor. We are beyond concern, even if we
believe the naysayers, even if we realise a strong apocalypse is good for the
    plant.
No, really, it ejected the dinosaurs last time, this time it might be us.
To make way for what, variegated leaf? We went wrong and now it must be the
epoch of the ant. When speaking of testing the (lack of) waters in order to
    move to Mars,
an astrobiologist says she wouldn't want to bring anything back she didn't
know she could personally kill if it threatened to kill us. Maybe we are dying
out to make way for that very Martian thing. Still, the patient sages of SETI
    listen out,
further out than puny Mars, for something perhaps still whispering there,
where there really is dark matter and black holes swallow up all the extinctions
we can imagine. Perhaps they even belch out new life; it depends how

narrowed your eyelids are when you glance at those glorious galaxies, those
stunning technicolour nebulas we coloured in.
Once, forever ago now, 1977, they did hear something out there: a lone
  frequency,
a perhaps-voice. That milli-second glitch. Since then, even when my
home computer joins in the search for things even beyond its ken, we still
  fumble over
far too many frequencies. Nothing is ever obvious or contained. How can I
  write a
lyric poem about the micro-needle in the gargantuan multiverse? The sheer
  size of
out there is beyond all possible thought about size in here. We are terrified of
all this expansion; we now devote our holy quest to the inwards, to breaking
  down.
With our Large Hadron Collider, we seek the sheer empty of within.
Within every final fragment, we dig deeper into beneath, towards the very
bowels of interior. There, inside the inside, past what we thought could not
  be broken down,
we think we might find a beginning, which is also our vast outside-end:
the future we saw when we were out there. We move outwards, inwards,
yet only ever see ourselves, mirrored inside our own vast solitude,
encompassing our own immense vacancies with more O-gape hole atomic
  space.

Fault

And the eye that looks out, this eye, your
eye, is cut by slanted light, slit by winter flowers.
You are caged behind glass, reading – reactor research –
reaching Fukushima, fearing it killing you here,
countries away, though only one continent.
Radiation sounds reminiscent of lost light, that
beatific bride on her day. Please don't mention the angels.
But you see your own removed tumour, deceptive cabbages,
future babies born with three appendages. Could be extra
heads, cut them off before the sea, the iodinated sea,
makes them more. No, that is a Kerberos myth fragment in your
ancient brain, not nuclear winter. There is nothing to fear
here, surely. Surely you know this, surely some demigod,
politics on fire, would have let you know, personally,
if there was room for fear this day. Yet for so long
the old gods, and even their bastards, have kept
silence like a last star in a box, stooping over it,
grey nomad phone psychics with Perspex crystal balls,
revealing nothing: too old for this game, using their
secrets to curry favour with the alien lords of the new galaxy
they will move on to, but you will not. The old gods
need their secrets to grant safe passage when this big star
spurts its final light seed and finally rots away.
At Fukushima, most were quick to blame those old gods for those
giant waves that broke the technology. Perhaps it was their last
blast before giving us all up and over to oblivion. Yet some are
not so sure. "When you inflict significant change to nature,
nature will eventually get back at you with significant force,"
says a scientist, the rational ones we hope will rule us now the old
gods are leaving for the parallel universe where nuclear technology

is a bad idea some evil priest had eons ago. They realigned him,
went back to singing together and dancing outdoors –
it's easy to correct faults there, in that parallel world.
Faults, in that place, be they of nature or nurture, can be
set like bones. In this world, at Fukushima, in the slightest review,
even with the help of the gods, faults in the system appear.
Faults appear but of course, they are as natural as air, and as necessary.
We cut twenty-five metres off a thirty-five metre sea cliff so
we didn't have to lift the seawater (a resource we make use of
because it's anyone's to use) too high, to power the power.
In lifting the sea too high, some multizillion dollar machine might
sprain its spine. It was the sixties, some world domination race or
another was on, humans were curious infants and you certainly weren't
born to be blamed for it. From what you can piece together, it was
all about getting through some awkward phase, the sixties, moving on,
and still remaining at the end. It was about continuing. It was
darker than Gilligan's Island lets on; there is something so sinister,
sending shiver, even now, in the phrase economic growth, even when
whispered in your mind by a shining image in an instamatic photo album.
Those endless albums your nanna had, with the plastic sticky sheets that
wrecked the photos in the end. In your more ancient bones, the ones that
mapped the world, created money and are always there, here and
everywhere, you know this truth like you've known nothing else:
Fukushima Power Station was built on the grounds of a WWII air base.
A colossal one. Nothing needs to be said about kook
recipes for what we all comprehend without enquiry. Spaces carry
gossamer fate snags, mapped out by the old gods (who are
leaving like the elves in Tolkien, see above). Fragments of this knowledge
must remain dormant in your bones even now like radioactive iodine.
Nobody mention the half-lives looming over us post-meltdown,
please do not say: sawing twenty five meters off a natural sea cliff is no
    small thing.
There is oh so much ocean for the isotopes to settle into; more everyday now

the great melt is on, and who are we to measure out boundaries for this or
   any
other inconvenience. This far and no further means nothing to nature.
This far and no further meant everything to the (recently departed) old
   gods.

Velocity

'Gustav was released off the Normandy coast and, faced with headwinds of up to 30mph and no sun to guide him on a cloudy day, he flew 150 miles to a pigeon loft in Thorney Island, near Portsmouth, in a journey that lasted five hours and 16 minutes... Gustav was the first of the RAF's Homing Pigeon Service to bring back news of D-Day to the UK.'

– BBC NEWS

And it's the birds again, their
Gossamer glory hooks tugging our
Eyes up from morning teacups

In the last leaf embers, we had been courting Doom

Yet gaze is raised up to Gustav
Flying WWII out of the Great Chronicle
Against all the God-fury we can imagine
The God-fury he no longer had to imagine
Over ghost ships and sea monsters

His own mass the only anchor: Hooked into sky

Because he had been directed
Because it was a sort of game
Because at the end if it all was a comfortable loft

At the end of our game
Remains the question: "who is best?"
It is not enough to simply regain home

We race on against devolution
Somehow settling the issue
Yet with each subatomic chaos-flux

Best is born again

In the white sky where it is finalised
Examples of endurance are thick as flies:
Gustav with his D-Day daring
And all the ghouls of the air

Here with us, mid-chase, through the not yet deciphered
Here with us, mid-chase, amongst the not quite decided
Here with us, mid-chase, inside the almost terminal

Breathless, we balance our pigeon post
Against one another:
A log chronicling the velocity of our Doom

"Who is best?" remaining our guide,
Residing inside the fracture:
Distance we have travelled to remain here
/
Speed with which we rush to regain home

Follies

Contact Juggler

Balanced on his shoulder like an extra atom, the ball is mirror is sea is your own mind. Please don't mention the emotional life. Even if you are on the outer surface of all of this inner poise, you are not so bad as the ball, the extra atom that nobody really bothered to make room for though they balance it there, though they remain abreast of it. There is no time for keeping still in all this avoiding the fall.

Even if you are the ball and the ball is not an extra atom, but is anti-atom, dark matter black hole – even this – still you must benefit from all this sucking it in, the great absorption of light. And, even better, through your quest towards down and off, you are necessary to keep the shining host where he is: onwards and upwards in mastery over gravity.

This is unlikely salvation, this exploration of the pretty parts of horizontal defiance. This is the contact juggler, the volatile element, on stage with that extra atom, circling the outer shell of skin, begging for ionic bonding, balancing immediacy over contraction.

Glass-Eater

It's killing you slowly but you don't mind. It's for the laughs or the money or the gasps or the tears or the squinting or the looking away. Sometimes the punters even leave the room – like that time you hung an iron off your nipple piercing. Too much, but that was the merest wince of body bombastic compared to the gawp of glass-eating. Perhaps you are secretly desperate for disembodiment after all. The crunch as it grinds around your gums is nails on blackboards. And I feed it to you under lights without question because you asked me to. Sometimes it's all miked up, as if happening were not enough, amplification adheres it to our adrenals. If the Fakirs had kept their mouths shut, if some long-held thought about God wasn't of an all-consuming grunt minus a body, if bodies were diamond, not her poor cousin carbon, this would be nothing. But even on a soft-lit stage with a cloaked smile, you are thin membranes and soft walls and squishy organs and if it doesn't get you today, there's always tomorrow's X-ray.

Angel of the Neo-Burlesque

Twigs and leaves going their separate ways like your brain against your mind: the great unfolding of matter from spirit.

What you are composed of – what is fundamentally unknown – will also one day leave this place, grow nearer to some elsewhere. You (the fundamental unknown) may even get there eventually, so you are told when they deign to tell the angels anything.

Moral philosophy? Of course you were lost to it! The ocean was just outside and there were mountains, inconceivable alps, kilometres beneath the surface, kilometres high. Best not to imagine the under-sea breadth of Sedna's smile or you'll end up inside it. Furthermore, her hidden fires, there, under the sea where magma meets the ocean deeps. Of course you had to don pasties, a diamante G-string and leap from the window, wings akimbo.

The soul must be wedded to the flesh. There is only this. You leapt.

Even now, you still peel gauze from your fingers, shards from the secret scars you gained as you charged through the glass. Even now, you (fundamentally unknown) pluck air and light from the sides of your eyes. Here in deep-sea, a shimmy is a sort of knowing, unfolding.

54 Working Murderers

For Major Barney, Newcastle Nobby's Breakwall, c1836.

'Major George Barney - resident civil engineer in charge of the Nobby's Breakwater project and a gang of 54 working murderers and hardened thieves - is hosting high tea for the Catholic Church on the lawn behind the Commandants Cottage. Abutting the copse a temporary platform has been erected and the town's finest string quartet are providing for entertainment. As the strings shrill and the players toil beneath tight collars, the sponge cake sweats in the afternoon heat....'
— *Bulletin*, 1836

This would be a lot easier if you weren't stuck forever between one point and another. If it weren't for God's endless chronology, you could be prised out, you could be given over to the now. You were at the colony to build the break-wall, but society ladies came first. Each gluon in this dot on what your lizard brain back then saw as a line but which we know now is really a broken hologram — history — displays the totality of the whole: Fifty working murderers and four hardened thieves, fifty Catholic ladies and four highly-strung instruments, all splayed through each slice, balancing each other out on the cosmic weighing machine. You probably don't even want this scene God thrust upon you: a shard of sponge cake, sweating in the sun. You eat it anyway, as we consume you - 1840, or perhaps today, it's difficult to differentiate in all this space-time quantum fielding. Your tastebuds expound the now rancid cream to your synapses, which pass the dire message like Chinese Whispers through neurotransmitters to your cerebral cortex but by then it is too late, Mrs Smith is asking what you think of her recipe. You may have never even met a Chinaman, let alone teased them over their mixed-up whispers, yet they are here already, near where we last imagined you, digging for gold dust, just around a corner somewhere. Mrs Smith casually mentions that the sweating sponge won first prize at the Parish Fair. You nod, but when she excuses herself it is spat out amongst the middens, against the bones of those you trespass across all summer long. The quartet covers over the clank of steel collars against chain. What is the ratio of cake to convict transpiration? Society ladies don't sweat, even when shipped from Brighton to Bloody Hell. The bones beneath no longer sweat. We still have lizard brains now, some seven score and more years later. For all their innovation, they can't begin to dream up this scene you didn't even want, the one God thrust out of the chronology, into the cortex of us all.

design

"The world is a corpse-eater'
– *Gospel of Phillip*

hesitant mauve against final cause red. jacaranda bows to the flame tree. sea hawk powers past. dog moans somewhere distant. dry wind cuts through dead snake grass. the cosmological decisiveness acquiesces to give you a seat in the scene. instead you rise.

you rise. too tardy for proper courtesy. introduce terms like teleological uncertainty to the morning. feel bad about it. continue on regardless. whims like intelligent design seep from the landscape. you roll your eyes. thread your toes through the pre-crushed petals. bleed more red. mauve deserves to be ignored. too reminiscent of society ladies.

camphor laurels are society ladies. they loom out there. nodding heads at fashionable dinners. chickens bob about in their run. they have not had breakfast. you have not had breakfast nor have you kissed your lover's forehead for days. the ocean you can barely see is out there anyway. constantly gobbling up shore. discretely so you barely notice. it is edging closer.

every day I realise we've left it too late to get it back, but then I work like a bitch to get it back. speaks a bush regeneration agent in the new day air. but you are scribbling. too busy for Sisyphus. lines turn into letters turn into denials you will never send. lack denotes longing. admission of longing assumes a fault somewhere. fault leads itself right down the garden path to blame.

there are billions upon billions of parallel worlds reclining just through that mauve and red. bathing just beyond that powdered baby blue and new leaf green. colours are veils. there are other worlds. just there on that other side. just get to them. just go. just get to one.

summer storm

isn't it 3.46am and aren't you standing in a storm-filled caravan. dancing to blondie with the symbols inside you somewhere. just under the skin. and didn't you at age twelve decide you knew where the blueprints to the right religion were. you simply had to imprint the inside surface of your skin out with carbon paper to get them. and then do it again and keep doing it until you understood. but eventually you would know. probably by age eighteen. well and truly by now. by now you would most likely be dead. you could still die right here right now in your annex. they put out the evacuation order and you don't have an operational phone. here with storm shakes and tree rattles. also steam and flame and other electric states you can't touch or even name the physical reaction to produce. not to mention that pause in the continuum all storms make. that glitch that keeps you remaining. here at 3.47am with all the copying instruments you need but no clue how to turn them on. or how to get them inside you. and still after all these years you fear you might rip your own spine out and sew it onto a leotard like sequins so they can all see right through the glamour to the blueprint inside.

l'escale restaurant

and it's not like you have some other place to be. tea, open fire place, open fire on some other space for avoidance. it's not like you are this ashes urn, portable picnic for later holocausts. or this charred log. you aren't even the small burning before the final ash out. most other people come here to support themselves in whatever horror seems most appropriate in which ever day dream. of theirs. this day. why not you. this time. possibly they realise you won't tip well even though lord knows desmond tutu ate here just last week. exclusivity should equal your absence. it's not as though anyone can shape this differently to how they were born to shape it. there are no other tools, no contrasting fashions, no further instructions. what does equality really signify in any case. an afternoon of missing your morning of the subsequent day means little here. sunlight so new and distant, almost reaching the sand inlet out the window before these clouds join forces to obfuscate it altogether.

LAX

Anaphase. You did ask for it. And now you're scared because it
smacks of chemicals. Beyond tired, Route 66 Roadhouse Café.
Since you can't begin to name the Presidents, what with all the
plane radiation and neon, this may not be wise. There's no point
postulating, time travel does something serious to your bones.
It comes to be only about gathering your pre-spindle DNA
fragments back together. It comes to solely be about sufferance,
clutching this airport lounge margarita as if it were a magnetic pole.

sky

like finally seeing the sky.
not seeing ourselves thinking
of the sky. just sky. blank sky
but for all this. if we read
more critical theory can we
possibly paraphrase or will
it do nothing but kill this
beautiful night. here where we
really are standing. fire clings
to the object that is being
consumed and thus is bright.
what is consumed. what is
oxidised. what is being-for-
death. what is re-arranged
re-arranges us as we partake
in shades. in segments. in the
trace. for the seeing being life
is a meaningful life. big with
the world above the artist
is speaking. we are nothing
looking up. out. finally seeing
sky.

night park

is there a tent of radiance to erect over this. a plastic bubble to lock in the child-smiles of day, block out the bad-lights, stark night. what if we begin to imagine what goes on here when the last swing surrenders to witching. sure, there is lamp-light. why does this evoke short, sharp, suppressed second-breaths. there is no live human presence left here to recount the tale, so why bother writing it in your mind. we know. this bench will not refuse to sing its sordid secrets, no matter what surveillance methods we pretend to use to pry them out. the community comprehends what really takes place in this public play space. when the lights go out, we shut our blinds to the myth, while the creek we really did name styx crouches in wait. a silent witness.

Senescence

'In modern scientific enquiry, the origin and nature of consciousness has yet to be fully understood; any... view about the existence or non-existence of consciousness after death therefore remains speculative.'
– Wikipedia

Probably I wake up and it is that first pause again: we are bold, glorious, probably made up of all these airs and swallowed dusts, only everything knows how beautiful – and still we do not die. How, as a child, I loved the sound of the word death more than the sound of life. Annunciating cessation: so exponential, the way the thhhh comes in at the end. If it is too crass to compare the resounding resonance to exhaled breath, I will write: the gift of pushing air out with the tongue. The gift of hiss. The hum of life, so flat and nasal-encumbered, while death is an upturned moon in the day-sky: a brush of unseen wing, never quite realised; our only secret. This early love of exponentials adhered the hiss of death to that virulent liquid coursing cushions between my brain and skull: the first sac where the last truth lies. That miracle: that I have not as yet died, though I have loved the sound of the word.

The Gaps

The text has holes in it, little keyholes for the sake of myth-making, and only the one star-gazing out can (im)possibly slip into them. There is a crucial adjustment when "how can I exist?" turns into "how can I be alive in this?" Suddenly those roundabout machines we built to keep ourselves way out of critical theory converge in the centre, provoking and awakening an idea of onwards-and-upwards. This sensation is momentary.

Even if I say to you "you are this if this is life" it won't matter and we will continue into cake at 3pm, our bodies refusing forever. Even if I sew in to my own skin the text: I will continue this remaining, the stitches will only remain, like me, until they don't anymore. When we need them to stay there forever.

To perform becomes the central verb. Like the encroaching creep of the sea, we now perform this abeyance as though this temporary pause to consider could be stitched into skin, as though that very same skin could push its way through all the gaps the text could (im)possibly hold. As though, at the end, that same stinking vellum could be stretched over contingency like a disappearance-blanket. As though we could then hide away under it, remain in this word: love.

Acknowledgements

Poems from this collection have also appeared in *Overland Literary Journal, Blue Dog Poetry Journal, Going Down Swinging, Mascara Literary Review, Voices from the Meadow, Swamp Journal, Five Bells, The Red Room Company's Pigeon Poetry Archive, Newcastle Poetry at the Pub Anthology, Sydney Writer's Festival: Poets Paint Words 2010, Newcastle Poetry Prize Anthology 2011* and *A Slow Combusting Hymn.*

Deepest thanks go out to Kim Cheng Boey, Keri Glastonbury and Brook Emery for constantly supporting my crazy notions. Many thanks also to David Musgrave and the crew at P&W for taking this long-lined manuscript on. Finally, I'd like to thank my wonderful family for utterly everything.